Looms

Also by Camille Martin

Sesame Kiosk
Codes of Public Sleep
Sonnets

Camille Martin

Looms

For Laurene
"We take our chances
passing each other hurrying
down shining streets,
umbrella grazing umbrella."
Cheers!
Camille

Shearsman Books

First published in the United Kingdom in 2012 by
Shearsman Books
50 Westons Hill Drive
Emersons Green
BRISTOL
BS16 7DF

Shearsman Books Ltd Registered Office
30–31 St. James Place, Mangotsfield, Bristol BS16 9JB
(this address not for correspondence)

http://www.shearsman.com/

ISBN 978-1-84861-235-8
First Edition

Copyright © Camille Martin, 2012

The right of Camille Martin to be identified as the author of this work has been asserted by her in accordance with the Copyrights, Designs and Patents Act of 1988.
All rights reserved.

Cover image (*Blind Man's Bluff*) by the author.

to my mother
for the gift of life and language

Its remoteness from the center of things is what is endearing about a Tale and it doesn't tell the truth about itself; it tells us what it dreams about.

—Barbara Guest

☙

Right now is what dwindling feels like, despite
the mulberry outside my window steadfastly
anchoring its taproot. The new century counts planets
that might support rooted beings and ravenous predators.
But stardust piles up on lines connecting dots
in constellations, blurring them into nebulae. Shapeless
experience waffles between concrete and abstract, accounting
for the popularity of horoscopes, especially when Jupiter enters
Aries and we vacillate, like volcanoes heaving ash
before the pyroclastic flow, collapsing before tsunami, dwindling
until the next cycle. I abstractly shake dew from ripe mulberries.
Or I lie down, gazing at shivering green tracery non-existent
a couple of months ago and just as soon to vanish.
A more or less concrete cup of coffee balances on my belly,
wobbling to the diastolic and systolic rhythms of my heart.

☙

To believe is to please what most you love, cruising
surface, catching strains of an old ballad
whose punctuation flickers like fireflies. Meaning
darkness, believable onyx in which crested memories
wander into a cascade. Of what? No one recalls,
but many have known roman numerals in black ink.
I believe I see them. I make them convincingly
cascade like tiny angular droplets, enough to . . .
I forget. But I believe I'm here with the beloved, each moment
fertile with cataclysm. If that's the only flaw, what's not
to believe? Habits levitate until land morphs into map,
flapping birds into street names. Zoom out,
zoom in: same catastrophic universe in which to believe
is to please. Zoom closer. One baby shoe perched
on a ledge. What happened? A smooth-talking
carnival barker magnetizes all his ducks in a row, pleasing
no one. Any belief will do, but every now and then
perfidy shows up with its pleasant molecules
and the baby just has to wait.

☙

Not all slopes are tragic. Sylphs propel delta waves
careening toward a valley floor, unearthing fossils
more enduring than the rock that embeds them. Debris
downshifts, yielding to free agents that activate selfhood's
dormant genes, flip the switch linking all by murex
to dye royal robes purple. Not all storms are deadly.
Riddles in calm light keep their secrets. Silver-tongued
thistles divine cyclones, release harbingers
of spiked flakes. Not all weather affects grain and rat
equally. A farmer sets his table and waits for poverty
to scavenge embroidery from famine. Not everyone
at the same time is hungry, some born to plagues of rust,
others to pealing bells. Not all the hungry awaken.
Some reach ether. Others concoct a scheme:
shred the map, ditch the crutches, torch the house.

☙

Re-inventing stairs takes a plot as subtle as dust
drifting onto a slope in undecided space: position
is everything. Even drifting stars imply a story.
Gather enough stories and some get buried forever
in urns. Those exhumed know that memory and sunlight
rove hand in hand, but they keep it secret. They know
that both weave their mirrors as loosely as spider webs
reflecting a clear sky shattered by more splashes than words
to describe water. As the saying goes, the lake shifts
its words in light of the hill. Shifting the alphabet is chancy
like the judicial system of a virus. How soon vapour
driven by chance forgets. Speech is soon followed
by rubble. The speaker remains hopeful
only to hear a familiar echo: "I am your voice
and I have your vote!" Fading echoes aren't the best
antiseptic, but isn't all life sacrosanct? Embellished
with disease, warriors long to understand,
but what they really want to fathom they kill.

☙

Night's pendulums rust. Penelope drops
a stitch, vespers nibble a shifting breeze, flies collide
with half-dreamt webs. Black bear and tundra
tumble down the well into sleep. Wings quiver
in quiet suspense. Spandrels breed more
spandrels for the involuntary ornament
of speech. Ebbing light's paralytic stinger
calms gravity fishing more gravity. Far
from desert, far from tropics, night blankets
the shade of a maple. Even the town crier sleeps.
I loiter and let whirligigs land, or navigate
fuzz floating toward shiny worlds. If I pantomime,
I lose detail, blurring the flame that lures moths,
gaining their figurative love. And though I offer
scant evidence, I unwittingly lay waste
to wide swaths of happy homes
and their stainless steel clocks.

☙

A tiny pronoun gestates under a full moon
beaming into a chamber. Forget
the enlightenment, forget the soundtrack
of a clockwork universe. A sweaty little god
parks his flesh on a telephone pole, panting
blessings on his nascent look-alike: "Bathed
in happy scraps, stunned and limbed
as you are, we anoint your salty room.
In your heyday, we'll climb trees with you
and spur the urge to pluck ripe
plums. In your dotage we'll rewind your key
until naïve blossoms once more adorn
dolls of dubious gender basking in the swoosh
of our endearments. Farewell to modesty,
you darling pout, goodbye to the intellect
of harpsichords. You deserve so much more."
His Chubbiness aims an arrow and releases, infusing
his would-be twin with the everlasting sorrow
of wrecked desire. "And now you of tender stuff
must practice with no discipline your blind
freedom, and I must flee to fertilize dry clay."
His job done, the imp flits away. The pronoun is ready
to kiss and scream its way with oily breath
into everlasting mischief. It wears the innocent
guise of the infant king, long gone and accepting no
responsibility, A sunny haze blurs genetics darkening
through its veins. It embarks flailing its arms, reaching
for its proper name to wield as it can,
schooled in cruelty by the best.

☙

A phantom cowers behind each thing stared at
but never seen, like a banana by its monkey. Lenses
drain the anvil's veneer, wipe the roof
of rain. A person flaunts a public pose but acts
alone, an extra in a movie about the sovereignty
of a bareback rider sporting a red cape
in a colouring book. Onto the set darts a warbling
mimus polyglotus repeating a phrase a few times
then never again. Idly picking weeds, we await
the hack from a film noir to careen
over a bridge after the detective shoots
the cabbie, barely alive but whispering to us
of a slicker lunacy, a blither kite.

☙

In the badlands of the vernacular, the talk is all
galactic halos misting retinas, fickle nymphs twirling
pinwheels. Pockets of silence, too, holding up soft mirrors
to wordlessness. Failure, shacked up with its rival.
Their coupling blurs the latitude dividing forest
from forest, haven to ferocious embryos that crack
their shells and flap into a menagerie where they can rouse
the most bedlam. Not the best place to ponder long-term
teleology, just apples and arrows, gadgets to open
containers of doubtful nutrition but undeniable
pleasure. This fattening up is ominous. One more bite
and I'll cross a border into realms where difference
is guarded by masquers. Impeccable their hunger, imperfect
their torches burning certainty as they sleep off three-dimensional
space. I create a predator and shoo it away. I clamber
after focus, pristine arts and letters, idols in limos,
mirages conjured by a jack-of-all-trades
with a love that triggers mutiny.

☙

Reaching the border, I forget why I came.
Must be for its own sake; the point seems
moot. It's a good place to camp and I can still see
out the window. I imagine the vista broader
here: I can quibble as long as I like. I know my disease
but only catalogue symptoms, like eyes the exact shade
of the clutter they invert. And my thoughts
having no passport, no crux, just background noise
to accompany their inevitable mistakes. Here
I can fail the Rorschach out my window, chatter endlessly
about rivers flowing upstream. Still at the border
in a dim room plunging headlong into omens.
I only know that a bit of sand makes a few marbles, that random
is just fingerprints, one planted on aging vellum,
the other on a coin spinning in soft light. Leaves
huddling next to my window last yellow
and fall, still filtering light on children at play.
It's a more ordinary place than I expected. I'd know
their little calls and yells anywhere, though it seems
I always hear them for the first time.

☙

Where peasants now hack at tough clods, a wharf
once jutted into shallows where kids caught sunfish
and threw them back into ripples lapping at rotted
wood. In the booming trade of myths, a paper plane sheds
pollen along a road where pages in a taxi's route once
floated out the window. Polaroid ibises peck holes
in papyrus while headlined runes guide the course
of their evolution. Breathed molecules feed into squalls
threatening scenic details, thin black perimeters defining
white lilies against foaming surf. You must retain these details
to be conscious, and each time you become yourself
it's the rapture all over again and you have to recommence
chanting and climbing hills. An old chorister recalls his songs
from youth, crisp and wild, but the chemistry never bloomed
the way he thinks it did. He can't read fine print anymore
and hears only dogs howling at the end of tethers.
He pedals a bicycle toward a castle whose nobles
have until now enjoyed bountiful harvests. He's desperate
to deliver his telegram: *This time around,*
the banners must be blue with a crescent moon.

☙

Scattering dust is good practice, like bouncing voices
off the wall, out the window into vapour. The future withholds
evidence, but if I wait long enough, dust will find
an upward drift, encounter fewer obstacles, unlike vision
blocked by tomatoes ripening on a stone or cranes arriving
to paint a rainbow. The colours are children who sing the same
nursery rhyme five hundred years later, rippling coded
sound waves into history. Something comes to pass that never
was, like the hum of a fridge, more constant than change,
more peaks and troughs than drops in a monsoon. It blends
with the music of the spheres and fritters into the rush of traffic.
I believe in a glass globe, lucid and fragile, but sprang
from mundane earth and walked, humbled to realize that mostly
I wait to carry trifles to another time and place and then be bled
as if to cure the recurring feeling of nothing left to do
but scatter dust, just in case.

☙

The focal point is off somewhere, sails propelled
by the buzz of cicadas headed who knows where.
"How blank," whispers the sun, swept into the undertow
such thoughts of absence lead to. The empty hold
echoes with voices of the last conversation:
"How clever we are, inventing land, mapping every
shadow. Was that really you guiding the flotilla
into a storm?" The drowned sun envies a wick's fate
melting wax into frozen waterfalls. What evidence
of rain? Cicadas envision silver fronds
flinging spores onto forest floors, blue
they will have the floors, and so begins a crescendo
of errors tilting mapped land until candles, targets,
brooms, boats, weather slide toward ocean
into impermanence. The ship sails into a storm
as witnessed. Cicadas and voices deeply converse.
The sun glides along a current, rises
at the next continent and peers downward
past clouds and v-formations to a pool
where a girl emerges from chlorinated water.
She turns her body toward the sun
and dries herself.

☙

An accident a thousand times is no accident. Nor
is it necessarily a plot. Homilies pierce the hearts of ideal
sheep, but thought starts elsewhere, as in perjury, as in
shuttlecock, as in the subtle architecture of a theory. Easy
tramping through mouldy corn, following shiny chrome
up a hairpin turn. Hard to cough up keys that free
empty cornucopias, warped funnels of zero. Lucky pixels,
hidden in plain sight from the overseer we love
to trick. His enviable trick: translate only errors and still
be legible. Thought starts elsewhere, as in homily,
as in pyramid, as in the climate of a blink. I'm held together
by stitches getting longer as I shrink, dancing
to the rhythm of my accidental fiction.

☙

They will take my island
to ukulele seas where mist coalesces
into petals laced with dew. I imagine already
hearing their cantabile swerve off
the chart into succulent winds. They make
me believe that, though we haven't yet
been formally introduced. I try
to make contact by floating a corked bottle
of cockles and musty pages toward
a cartoon etched in my brain of a ragged man
marooned on a neighbouring island poring
over a treasure map. They patiently
acknowledge my attempt. I'm forever
late scanning the horizon, so here's
where I have to dig. But what island?
In what sea? Which me pumps the treadle
that spins the gears that keep the zodiac
mentally wheeling across the big clock?
This is what I know: I exaggerate
their finessed vision, their exploded view
of every grain of sand. Such compliant
metaphors, these grains on which I circle
along the mundane fractals of my shoreline
guided by shape-shifting constellations.
My island is trained in the arts of prisoners
dragging red herrings to dead ends
and splashing through the middle of creeks
to throw off the dogs that never
evolved here anyway. They know that.

I eavesdrop on their prattle fathoms
under distant fishing boats. By the light
of my remaining candles I carve
tools from native trees as wax puddles
on the volcanic rock that shaped
my island. They will take my island
to that melted wax.

☙

Old songs are either forgotten
or conned. Wired zygotes already spout
clichés. Even contagion wreaking havoc
travels predictably well. On cue, thought spatters
into as many beads as trinkets under a child's bed.
Until it dissolves, a crow swoops, combs
drafts, surveys cradled earth. Wind evokes
the billowy myth of curtains. Dying light
sweeps framed atoms. What I wish for
is unclear. No need to backtrack, but the crow
lands on a limb it doesn't resemble. The limb
dozes under drifting snow, succumbs after dusk
slumps. I wish to find one more category to undo,
but already I wander into a sea commissioned
by shipwrecks, shore awash in the briefest
of haunts. Flashback: from a treetop, a crow
nosedives, bathed in lapsarian rhythm. Fly-by-night
letters leave traces on calendars. Today reads
dovetailed mist. It hardly matters what I wish, but still,
curling waves laced with foam shift grains. Orbits
tilt in clueless rooms. Shards of colour tumble
onto mirrors in rolling tubes.

☙

I remember zero in the dark, personhood
embarking on a leaf skimming surface
tension. I remember falling asleep in bankruptcy
and dreaming a flawless edition, romping
in euphemisms. I remember a banquet for decoys
and their cold internal clocks, syntax gauging rich
absence. I remember spurning abacus, crossing
my sobriquet with marsh flowers growing in cracked
soil, clumps of clay, fertile valleys. I remember plundering
paper boats, drowning suns, burning a wick in a fake
lamp, unravel becoming the norm. I remember games
of painting over escape hatches while deserted smoke rings
hit the wall and vanished. I remember the broken record
of a skipping needle, oboes echoing sad riffs, redundancies
waving their dizzying streamers. I remember pronouns
hacking verbs, bloodthirsty animals dressed as humans
in ballet shoes. I remember zero in the dark, abandoning
sails. I remember the comfort of madeleines, of counting steps
along a trail. I remember storybooks, sunbeams
flickering through bare branches guiding children
home, rhymes of sprouting leaves planting memories
of a feast, roots anchoring until even the refrain believed
the way things might still be. I remember remembering
now, melodies gathering into clusters of grapes, cold feet
warming under a quilt, holiday secrets, little jokes
of childhood, weather spiralling counter-clockwise.

☙

Let's pretend, though our philosophy
limps. A dragonfly constellation flickers
through a skylight. Someone snaps
a photograph to simulate the room. Quaking
bedrock jolts reason contemplating the journey
of plankton through ocean currents. Over whitecaps,
winds buffet feathers. Feathers buffet parrots
to no avail. Plummeting parrots tell their own
tale: children wandering through woods
toward a warehouse elevator that shuts out light.
Blood-sucking shepherds roam steppes. No hope
for movies or zombie genetics. Try again.
A gunslinger swaggers out a saloon to change
the light bulbs of cacti. A doll takes his place
playing poker. Tiny creatures curl up
in the men's ears. A hush falls over the saloon.
Guard-rails rot as the elevator glides along
a catwalk, ruminating, "Would it be a terrible
mistake? Pagodas over pine cones?"

☙

No one wants to break the storm of habits
the experts claim won't change anyway.
So we have the satisfaction of being right
and safe, hiding behind our galactic shrine
of choice, fastening bows on silhouettes. It's time
someone shoved a mountain. Too much at stake
to prove him wrong. Winning's written into the outcome.
And so he wins, to no one's satisfaction. We suffer
the end of solidity and call the breakthrough the last
heist, the definition of a defining moment, an explosion.
Or a pebble plucked from sand. A filament
has been crossed, and all struggle to recollect
what storms do. On the moon, a cricket perches
on a crater's rim and leaps into the colossal scar, severing
the link with its earthly double, which thereafter
longs for the impact of foreign bodies
and the hollows of scooped melons.

☙

Remote suns. Must be tale-spinning feeds the music
of their slow-motion flowering dependent
on gravity. During harmonic change, chords
briefly overlap. In the dissonance,
scampering mobs rise and also subject to gravity
tumble. Insects, forgotten in the turmoil.
Their colours wouldn't work in the new world,
where people learn that it all boils down
to salt, and each has in mind a different brand of salt.
Some won't last, despite boastful jingles. Lovers
long to choreograph love scenes unblemished
by ads, a cherished memory now as distant
as ancient musical modes whose actual
scales and subtle emotions allegedly stirred
can only be guessed. The ground cracks
open, flanked by rows of crops. Out soars
a chariot ferrying gods to plot their heist. Harvest
begets cavalry begets merchants who buy their offspring
leisure to study ancient feelings—manliness, melancholy,
erotic love—and recompose lost music all because of
renewed faith in anything from fireworks to rotting
mulch. And though the progeny never publish
these hymns to their rage for marrow,
distant suns hum the tune.

☙

Lunar flutes waft cool wind on the skin
of a planet endearingly obsolete
from the outset. Time flutters, farcical
in tin-pan light, gravel tumbling in a barrel.
Olden taxis dither on pontoons. Briny moon,
cratered sea, triumph of orange stork in a dynamo
of speckled eggs. Rusted bridge, lullaby. Butte
with jutting cliff, lullaby. Lawless cobras, oddly
mellow, nudging lilies awake. Sleepless
cosmos with bells and a bird's-eye view melts
into mock embryonic flux. Cloud, crowd,
where have you been? Following landmarks
with lost bearings, mapping the genome of empty
baskets, galloping to Valhalla on a pinkish-yellow
ray. If leaf, then arpeggio. If sand,
then arabesque. Lazarus never had it so good, half
winged, half drunk, rattling the bars of his dreamed
cage with nothing to keep him but ripening
garlands, flaming hoops, swans on ice.

☙

Gliding through arteries you arrive naked
and vulnerable at the brink of a cliff. An oracle
dares you to roam faraway lands to learn
whether ballooning junk status can foster social
cohesion or whether Oedipus really needed
to know. Indifference is a country where trees dream
of primitive cells parading to the common ancestor
from which flora that would later look good
on someone's mantle branched off. Here, a twitch
is a cup waiting to spill. If your evolution begins
at the finish line (which it won't,
but that's not the point), jump from the cliff
down a hole to the other side of the earth
and start over again naked and vulnerable
at the brink of a cliff.

☙

Mallets ring the alphabet down
to "xylophone." But the glissando through the air
might be just more air filed away under "solemn"
or maybe "cartoonish." Tiresias turns heavenward
with all the blindness of a coattail ride. Godhead
can't target a muggy day. Hovering between,
a tennis court net, a quiet diary entry that never
says the first thing about indigo buntings,
always just around the corner. Into the gap
solar pulp lows across a tinsel podium
on a mountain peak, describing a sublime
panorama, boasting of harvesting valley trembles
to feed a falsely-worshiped zenith. Rays ad-lib
through leaves onto aphids whose honeyed
allegories render blight visible. On the verge
of blowing their cover, they welcome
the arrival of night as coy as indigo buntings,
always just around the corner. The irony
of autumn is a gilded song.

☙

The flame that I would bring would not
be something I remember having read,
not a replay of grief with revisions lofty
as a change of rein. For you are my firstborn,
premature, struggling to be free of accumulated
scenery. Memory has eluded me till the present,
hidden in fields gone to seed. Optimism brims
with purpose to bear a denial toward someone
playing the last hand of a card game. Sorrows
pronounce themselves because blood continues
to pump, peering through our skin and the shield
of our voices. I remember the name of one colour,
that is, what you bring to it, the way interruptions
collide, the serenity of one over the other.
This heritage where my mitres don't meet occurs
somewhere off the page. And even though we don't
talk of it under a steady barrage of dead signs,
we turn against our words when sleeves touch
in a state of careless grace.

ೋ

It speaks the shifty language of sluggards
who spill primer on aurora borealis, never imagining
their dissonant grammar shapes the cold. It cares
nothing for an exploded view of itself. It's already bribed
its hagiographer and hunted down the correct cobblestones
on which to have been born belting orphic arias
into posterity. Catechized at the cult of memory,
its customs lasso face muscles into a caricature. It's unable
to fathom that it has more dreams of rivers per minute
than droplets in the stagnant pool of its lexicon.
The instant it looks away, everything changes,
but it has no strategy to keep up. The blooms it inherited
a little smeared, a little parched, it gives away larger than life.
It's generous that way, if ignorant, spreading frayed
stories with auras. It listens to marimbas for hours,
yet marimba means nothing to it. It steals
or as it puts it, "absorbs." It brays of the powers
of its dogma and screws its head on tight.
But how many deathbed confessions will it take
to throw out the baby? It loves to repeat
the simple truth that it lives in a city on a lake,
but its portrait hangs in a dim hall
under a lapsed roof.

☏

The ship tilts and sinks, settles on ocean floor.
Without warning, the tale ends. Such larvae of habit
we are. Snow joins more snow falling on debris
(according to stage directions) but nowhere near the stage.
Winter's thought blankets camouflaged owls. Hard
for humans to cobble together what's already
finished. But they do, all aflutter with plans, big
plans, for the penultimate act. *The ship begins to list,
fills with water.* If only it were a case of bad acting,
pretending not to have change, all the while plucking
pennies from the sidewalk. I'm good at blaming
others, even when I know I'm culpable. But it's you
who concerns me now. *The swaggering ship needs no
belief. It defines itself.* Drops fall from a leaky ceiling
into buckets that overflow, portending an abundant
harvest. Let idle thoughts echo from room to room,
for whoever made the shibboleth can't pass
their own test. They describe knots without seeing
the horizon. But the big picture sees them, and soon
they forget how to cry over spilt ocean.
The ship tills the waves, lilts on salt water.
They won't turn on you. They are sympathetic
little calamities, if unsettling, as if wind needed
a reason. There is no heart of the world.
Here comes another planet. *A new ship sets out
in fine fettle. It flits and weaves. It bows
and lifts. It awes the sea.*

☙

At our uncouth birth the cosmos exhausted
names for hucksters presumed extinct. We shun
geometry while bisecting trapezoid spirals. It never dawns
on us to stockpile ephemera for a hard-up
day. Spotlights might stop some felons,
but not us. We toss our sabots into the rapid reflexes
of clocks, pinch diamonds and fence them for a fleeting
pair of eyes. We lie in wait for ourselves, birdlime capturing
a warbling feast. We breed depth, skim surface,
plunge into deafening throngs and spring back. From banal
atoms we conjure apocalypse and spurn mop-up operations.
We are castaways in limbo with artificial wings and no
aspiration. Pressed to find a flaw, we say we're failed
meteorologists wandering from puddle to puddle,
spooning up the rain to read the sky.

☙

Between grass and vacuum, standing on faded
tapestry in a low cloud, the odd pine cone skittering down
a roof. Some burgeoning belief poses—index finger raised—
and then *that* becomes life strolling down a parallel road
beneath a gentle sky, a cruel sky. Consoling
to think of burning ballast for light, brewing letters from ashes
moistened with a little fog. If all weather reports of one life
redeemed emptiness, maybe the ordinary could re-emerge,
inert, forgettable, except for the part where it juts and struts
and sobs. Worth a try to con it with words of practiced
lust settling like dead metaphors on scrap. Easy to love
indelible ink, gliding down opaque roads. But to ponder it
is to falter and to falter is to reawaken standing on faded tapestry
now different somehow. If I could sugar-coat one tiny historical
diva of a moment as the last rose on earth withers. Then *that*
becomes the reigning prophesy. No way to grasp unique
blades, so they vanish with or without exegesis
into static. With no motive but moving limbs, pedestrians
absorb bland gravity and step on soft signals.

☙

I arrive at a friend's house.
We look at magazine pictures.
Outside, the wind howls.
Morning lights a sliver of orange dream.
I drive along the sliver and hit a patch of mud.
The car sinks, just like in real life.
I climb out and walk to a friend's house.
We look at magazine pictures.

☙

At the denouement, crops like clockwork
fail. The master of origami folds and re-
folds his brainstorm of a cloud seeder, the arc of every
test flight a chink in gravity's attention deficit.
Outlaw aerodynamics brings muscle memory into focus:
dotted lines, precise repetition of erratic pleats. Minor
characters improvise buzz of easterlies bearing red walls
of dust, silt of past perfect finales sifting through sieves
like long-awaited drizzle through fingertips.
A farmer drawls his arid soliloquy, fist cursing
the backdrop of crumpled white puffs accented
with delicate brushstrokes of cerulean. The great folder
of mobile critters mounts his latest masterpiece
and teeters into the yonder, earnestly yanking
the neck and tail of his flappable plane.

☙

A mockingbird flies through an open window
toward light. Always the same troubadour, never
the same song. A castaway seeks land, anything
to call solid, rowing toward cloudy masses
where a pioneer whittles a stick with a sharp iron tool
before orders arrive to chop cypresses blooming with egrets
to make space for buildings. In one, an insomniac wades
knee-deep in archives, contemplates rejoining his own era,
finding a clone to view his haunt from outside. Inside,
heart connects to muscles wringing ink from night.
Dipping a finger in black fluid, he traces loops and swirls
of willows undulating in the breeze. Each ribbony leaf
cuts into the veneer of anything it's not: thunderous
blue, movement on greased wheels, iconic turf colonized
by visionary creatures evolved beyond recognition
who wait by windows for the mockingbird's arrival.
Even the least subtle perceives atoms vibrating
in the cranium of the bird that swoops into the house blazing
with commemorative lights. The bird warbles the news:
hominids are now deliberately striding over hill after hill
toward vast sweeps of magenta and gold.

☙

Welcome home. That was a lie. A well-worn
road crosses the gate. You can't stop
running in place, but at least you know
you're in the tale, as opposed to dangling
over a trap door unaware that your character
could slip away any moment. You understand
your origin in snake oil. More lies of a jester
twisting gossip. Who'd want to stem the propaganda?
Under the skin, it maintains the rhythm
of mechanical birds. Therein dwells a queen
in quarantine, unable to avoid plaguy rats
or to stop running in place before the gate. "Lies!"
she mutters. "Lies and crusades to more convincing
mirages!" In her head, discord driven by *basso continuo*
reminds her of dithering along a shore spying
the ship she's to arrive on but never does. She's embroiled
in the wrong heraldry, so long has she heeded
the spinning of her scribes. Which is to say
lies of lackeys absorbed in their own picaresque.
The queen fades as her jester looks on. Be sure,
she instructs, to linger around the battlefield, save
the scraps after the clashes. Then she's gone. Welcome
home. Lingering is impossible. Deceit tunnels
underfoot as you put your shoes on in the morning,
start to walk, open your mouth to speak.

☙

Thread, I follow you into the headlights
of dawn, witness panes reflecting clouds crooning
poofy hymns that signal little but inchoate thought
and drops captured by an overdeveloped earth. The thread
snaps, and seeing no signpost, I lose my way. Circling
in the woods I meet it again, floating in the vague rain
summoned expressly for thick-petalled bog flowers.
Crepuscular orchids, what's the point navigating
by your pigments bled of traceable empire?
What signifies a feathery voice while engines rev?
It's already light. Chalk scratches lousy
arithmetic, melted forest lies resolved, flat green
recalling pungent stories of lovers. I awaken
to a bird posing as a lark and follow
the looping tether of its song to the end.

☙

A speck of dust on the petal of a plastic mum shelved
beside figurines with flowering navels. They hold vigil
as dawn stirs over the river and people shift
in earnest. Roof after roof shelters hands held in rings
of rapport but for certain shades of cornflower blue
and fuchsia, tinted dust settling on tchotchkes waiting
on the shelf. The hand-holders fear they'll never really
know each other, patients in a waiting room each
with unique symptoms and prognoses. Like their shelved
treasures, the patients keep vigil, spiralling small talk
down to shuffling shoes, mentally cataloguing
the items on their shelves. None admit to awaiting
revolution. But each believes it might begin any
moment, a pupa nestling in a crate of grizzled roots
on a barge drifting to shore.

☙

A deserted city. We'll have to imagine
it's in a movie. Beneath a listless dome, walls
crumble into backlit dust. Flames on a hillside swarm,
tattered auburn fishes in the autumn wind. Glints of dying
light fall on unmoored mountains whose thoughts of home
come to nothing. Everywhere, flocks of matter dip pale snouts
into inky ponds. We'll have to imagine someone watching
that movie. No one left to forget irrelevant seeds. Some left off
praying to the mother of a tarnished idol presiding over a flock
of angels, breath attended by golden lice. Others
paused long enough to view dusk's leisurely descent
over the white noise of crashing surf. All found *something*
to swear by before it was too late. Photogenic dullards jazzed
in the waning light. A ship's captain jingled his coins
before staving in the ship. Embers in a hearth
illuminated fish bones on plates.

☙

Mumbling math for caravans rolling from apples
to oranges and back again, syllables blurred
by brushstrokes. He might have opened and shut
doors aglitter with constellations of clipped
Cassiopeian wings, hallooed criss-crossing dogs eager
with the scent of wastrels dispersing fear
through brambles, saluted undying accidents born
of plumage turning verbed orbits into truth-telling
cash. Instead, he searches for himself along halls
of marble pried from mountains focused
on the canopy above random limbs gliding
through displaced air. Droll, the portrait
quietly hoarding light and sound, mindful
of the possibility of one thought knowing itself
within the polyphony of bells that gleam
against a sky awash in red pigment.

☙

Paradise used to be solemn arpeggios accompanied
by flakes of snow. A child, I collected broken glass
and wondered whether tomorrow the clock
would begin ticking in earnest. Tomorrow hoisted
its flag and I surrendered the shards. So much
for windows. They hadn't yet lured light. Brushes
dipped only in grey. I was far away in a tale
set in nondescript climate. The etcetera fairy nested
in my cortex and inscribed the story with invisible
ink. I heard the soliloquy of cloth worn down
to a thread. I scraped scales from fish with a knife
whittled to a wisp. Above me, wings carved space
into a single quill. The fairy always left unresolved
moments. The moments coalesced into a plot,
which had learned from long experience to limp
on a prosthesis more vaguely defined than rot.

☙

History urges heroism or some such pulp, bustles around
with sponges and pots, occasionally offering something
like a year of birth, but not so intimate. Indelible water
records a slug's take on the universe, starting
with a drum roll. The slug drools with syntax imagining itself
limpid, thinking to trek as the crow flies. Semantics
torques between lip and phoneme, and superstition coats
the banal. Banking the plane into uncertainty might be a relief
but just in time, a clarinet solo pierces the atmosphere
like a cedar waxwing pecking red berries in snow. Analogies
fail the test of superfluity, and spring packs extra lapses.
Cold rain patters on a phone booth's roof, drowning out
the reedy d-flat in the dangling earpiece, Arcadian relic
fallen into disuse. Telepathic scribes periodically vow
to phase in cameras but promptly forget
and continue scribbling their blur.

☙

Theories await song birds at eye level for the clarity
of fresh lungs, torched crops. Phobias twist probable
cause. Under a salvo of colour, grapevines climb
to black holes. Favourite superstitions sift through scree
at the base of a cliff. Walls bolster habits,
guesswork crumbles walls. Clocks rewind
to a legend over which wizards cast obsolete spells.
Fishers reel in paranormal boots. Buildings
topple, ransom for already-devoured grub. Vague feelings
ready wishful song. Gardeners plant rust.

☙

Leaves die, but tangents conspire. I watch
an unlikely sunset from the shadow of a mountain.
In the time it takes to say "double petals,"
winter arrives, or an imitation. I've pocketed
the keys and jangle them, marvelling at their sheer
number and pointless blades. Monuments tempting
iconoclastic souls expand and topple.
Decay frequents alleys and rats. My gullibility
is boundless. Seasons parade fossils, leaves make
fodder. No planets for them all, so they burn luminous
pastels, having witnessed corrugated fields before seeds
were sown. These hollow sleepwalking colours
blow. Clouds nest between branches as window
and snow bandy inklings of light.

☙

What-ifs involuntarily search
for stained glass, antlers, gangplanks. No mistakes
yet, only intuition stewing in an age that fantasizes
technology making us immortal and foretells disasters
of mass extinction. Hammers and things that can't
be hammered. No landmarks for tides to wash away,
just shape-shifting topiaries throwing shadows
that glide to the rhythm of successively bigger
dramas. Sundials know what's in store
but they cast plots anyway. Enter choice, wandering
into a lake of feathers in rising wind.

☙

My yellow plastic horses melt
on a sidewalk. From a jetty, I watch
a parhelion sun slip into a lake. Another selective
autobiography, inviting rain and continental drift
to wash away craters. Weather never bothers
the horizon, just leaves it lying there composite,
unmemorable until I'm in the eye of a cyclone
waiting for the wall of wind to smack.
Or until I spot the distant sheen of olive trees
from a tower's vertiginous height. Then, horizon
sprawls, connecting cardinal points below
the solo moon, happenings threaded, one room
causing another, morning dissolving into dusk, tower
into clay roofs into olives into horizon.
Somewhere lurks the plague, but maybe
you can't get it on a rainy night, immunized
by the first flamboyant thing to enter your head,
half-empty for all its bruit. We take our chances
passing each other hurrying down shiny streets,
umbrella grazing umbrella.

☙

It's hard to give birth to prisoners doomed
to obsess over weather and complain
about traffic, difficult not to rate their ranting
parts of speech avoiding difference. Their hindsight
duplicates fruitless anthems, and mundane
vanishing points come and go between birth
and whenever now is. Hard to face toothless
light-years, table settings frozen in time. Ennui blossomed
before the first rock shattered, before it was even
rock, before cold starlight shone on exploded life forms
putting stylus to papyrus. The scroll opens to the same place
every time: same question, open-ended reply, then another
question, friendly feuds between indifferent wavelengths
prattling inmate slang stripped bare. Bones dangle
from strings clacking in wind that rushes over the shadows
of ants crawling on ant-sized paths without
the tempering passion of mercy.

☙

Wild creatures creep from artificial
woods. They're done climbing ladders and rigging
periscopes to see outside, and long to cross the divide
splitting vision down the middle. Maybe
it was landscape's fault—crags to the west, plains
to the east. One side relates to rock, the other *is*
rock, more being than backlit ghost. Stone's weight,
egg wash. The creatures have followed paths
without quite knowing why, swallowed their own
fables, fancied themselves unique. Stumbling into
monotonous light, they blink a shock of smooth slate.
Their species is finally getting somewhere, though none
have yet learned the possibilities of the song
they swing like a bludgeon.

☙

Distance means nothing to a map inventing crises
for a pilgrimage to a rippled lake on which to skip
pebbles. The map offers the pilgrim faith to believe
the ripples and vision to penetrate the murky water
in which algae breed before geological time serves up
predators. The organisms rediscover lost languages
in pockets of urban density, dream of shades destined
to wander in libraries, ghostly fast-forwards in search
of origin, declaiming the first word of each book, always
disappointed: "That's not it," the phantoms cry.
"There must be a start, and the start must have the clarity
of itself. Open the gate!" they command, knowing well
there's no gate to open. They're stuck reciting
the rosary of their era, a guide to compulsive hoarding
infinitely to recreate the moment of their birth.
On the map, a long journey and much to forget.
The pilgrim stoops to drink.

☙

We're hardly aware when migratory birds slip
away to the south, as though a thief
had cut the anchor and quietly sailed away. A book
pretends to decipher migration but sleeps
through winter in oblivion. If I'm not asleep
now, then my solace is dubious and the slippery
deck an invisible fate. The slumbering book's
birds cleave the wind and share their thieved
itinerary with painted waves. The horizon is a thief
stealing ships without anchors. In their roving sleep
ships decline the comfort of familiar books
and under full sail rejoin their doubting fleet. Slips
of paper slip from the hands of thieves who fall asleep
as subtly as migratory birds in a book.

☙

To measure the altitude of the moon, start
with zero degrees. Prepare a goo
by heating linseed oil in a pot. Meanwhile
cut out a rectangular piece of cardboard.
With goo attach a drinking straw
along the bottom of the cardboard.
Slip a washer onto one end of a length
of string. Tie the other end to your finger.
Swing the plumb bob for about two hours. Untie
the string and thread it through the hole of the straw.
Finally, tie a knot at the end of the string
and carefully balance the rectangular cardboard.
This is your tightrope walker.

☙

My reflection in the shiny pot startles.
Its twin spills water on the kitchen floor
and reads the iterable signature of dirty feet
that don't seem to belong to it: *les pieds*. Breaking
the spell, it swings from the light fixture so vigorously
as nearly to miss the pause-worthy schooner loaded
with *rosa muscosa* floating by. The sailors have brought
horticulture, their intentions bound to be misunderstood
in light of historical baggage, images from their voyage
destined to be stylized in three-colour silk-screens
in fifth-grade history textbooks, pink slightly off-
kilter. The historian moonlights as the writer
of onomatopoeia in Batman comic strips. *Fwap!*
for the slugfest inside Robin's head. Robin
is fighting for the freedom to wander with rootless limbs,
or to keep slugging away.

☙

Flagrant blue and green, smooth as a baby's
earlobe. The sun taunts, "Pretend you don't exist, barring
your bootless words. Now who reaps jigsaw puzzles?"
Windows! Something's lost in translation
and we're tempted to repeat in drops of rain and dance
the dance described in a text bubble. *Windows!*
This morning I slipped in a puddle of milk, but where
did it go? A prognosticating horse, where did it come from?
Windows! Muddy, streaked, crystalline. I say hello
thousands of times a day. Colours pop against
colours they can't see. I greedily hoard broken
toys in the hold below deck. Then I swab the deck,
listening for toys to follow tradition gloriously.
But will they still be toys? If puns like surfacing, why
are they grouped with heartbeat or breath? *Windows!*
They flatter, they scatter seeds in a vacuum. They recall
Tuscan vistas painters die for. They whisper,
"Who opens me opens," all the while hoarding
dim future in broad daylight.

☙

As people think, rain falls, reviving dormant
kudzu that climbs walls, swallows houses
where they crouch, people where they think. People move
to new towns, abandoning thought that creeps
and intertwines with kudzu, tendrils and reveries
twirling aimlessly down empty streets. Dogs howl,
inviting more howls to rescue thought with sonic
rope. In vain. Here come the vines again, devouring
staircases, acting as if they belonged
to the animal kingdom. People return to claim
their thoughts, now entangled with kudzu camouflaged
as brick and mortar with the cunning of a beast
that wants only to survive.

☙

Senses brave another day painting tropes
of rigor mortis, lullabies blanketing fields of yellow
that'd make you cry. Under surges of white noise
senses confess and hibernate. Drained of colour, goldenrods
elude charted continents and their slick embrace
of consciousness. They inhabit decay as senses import
pleasure—perfume, brandy, pastel porcelain lovers—
filtering untapped shades. But some crises
of blending can't be helped, like when Earth collided
with Theia and we're belatedly absolved of complicity.
We cannot see without bellies but long
to stroll through thickets, unafraid to call
what our senses don't love, home.

☙

Cars rush through precarious towns on a network
of simple arrival, follow legends of blue and red
strands, overdetermined but mute. Residual colours
rotate into weather that never quite attains a sum
but urges gusts on the windshield with a dull whistle
sunlight slants to. Non-stop highways unfurl dwelling's
non-sequiturs, homecoming around every bend. Yesterday
closes in, starting from scratch to shape a vision
of home as what and where, a point of reference, recognizable
despite endless variations of chair, window, robe
outlined inside a sealed colouring book.

☙

Nostalgia came later. Fishes at large
in their cold sanctuary dream that nets evolve
into willows. Linnaeus on a jetty waits for indecipherable
organisms to become relevant. History coaxes waves to focus
on plot (zebras, alert on the open savannah) then dissolve
into the afterbirth of shells. But earth is a thorny palette.
Below the crust and up in the ether, it's easier
to blend shades, melt stripes, claim as many symbols
as letters in our perfectly adapted alphabet. We deduce
that who we are depends on how we ask the question
and who asks it. Mutation all over again, each time slightly
altered, mispronouncing a word to re-imagine its gist.
But whispering a rumour isn't the same as inheriting it.
We suspect that in ancient blood courses the possibility
of owning more than home, of running in packs
of prosthetic power. That the postures of enshrined bones
prefigure our own guarded terror of the other.

☙

Bewilderment strolls down a dead-end
alley through cottony plumes overflowing
from buckets of dry ice. A gumshoe yearning
for the scenic archipelago he deserted yanks
blinds up and down. Flickering light enters
multiple apertures across the street where men
with contorted faces gaze at an abandoned
suitcase their nemesis crammed with desire. Limbs,
always belonging to the other, slice through mist
the ocean liner on a nearby set calls fog.
When the double-dealer awakens, she'll recollect
neither black and white contrast on walls
nor looser shades of leaf on moonlit
stone, but conspire to shoot her lover
in natural light. Her amnesia flashes images
of blinking neon stars once viewed from a porthole
and the silhouette of a man cast onto billows
soon to overpower him. His last thought:
wind banging shutters against a dump. Flashback
to crosshairs focused on the tinted glass
of a black car. The deed must be done now
or never. Light flickers at the edge of a lens, a signal
to squeeze the trigger of a pistol aimed
at a stranger's counterfeit heart.

☙

Nocturnes of elbow room within
elbow room, fathoms of protozoans
come full circle. Fireflies orbit, illuminating
blank curves. Silhouettes glide
through cold rain seeping into an empty
birdhouse. Nascent mind creeps along its blueprint
as muscles reach with the twitchiness
of a hair trigger dawn. Hunger strides
from ocean, palms above water above sand.
Lungs fill, spurred by fleas biting tiny
apples. Clappers await sound waves bunched in copper
suspense; heraldry awaits rank. Closed eyes
envelope violet, delicate icicle, envelope thorn.

☙

Streets flood. Elsewhere, sleet settles on mud
during the darkest night of the year. Hindsight orbiting
a crystal ball comes full circle. Imagined scenes, each
more prophetic than the last, gather no moss. A stage
lights up. Enter chorus, crooning the clairvoyance
of rising curtains, aiming for an emotion of incurable
gossamer. Viennese operetta: a lieutenant gazes
at the shore littered with relics destined
for pawn shops. At the denouement, high tide sweeps
across the stage, drives audience and players
into flooding streets. But I digress.

☙

To see is artificial, and artificial tears
wash away dead leaves, letting dandelions
grow anew. When Pluto peers through a needle's
eye, when atoms quell their circuses, then rough
air once more rushes into lungs, and desert grit
drips in an hourglass buried deep inside
the brain. Skin melts rock. Rock fools
birth. Seeing is still artificial, almost like flowers
glued into a vase. Almost like flowers, the dandelions.
But not quite. Eyes are especially vulnerable
to venom and belief. In their inbred delirium
they see weeds. Preening sham feathers, they repeat
the error until blindness isn't a choice
but just another belief. They row the light,
they bail the air. With chalk they cannot see,
they sketch fibres on a fossil's thorax. Their rays carve
monsters of winter psyche. They demolish buildings
mid-construction, offering artificial flowers
in their place. Wrong but true to their game they brim
with hope at the finish line. The finish line is aware,
just aware and little else.

☙

Red socks on an orange rug coax the next
self-portrait with barbaric bouquet. On a slackening
earth, the ghost covets what's too late
to be grasped—a pair of dice, a smoking
wick. Timekeepers add a second to fix the Big Dipper
in place: gears keep a cloud of gnats afloat, amoebas
gnaw lengthening days to bits. Late for thought, light
bounces up to the eyes of a pilot who lands in a tangle
over an emerald sea. He dives in, snags
a current urging the next crisis: an iceberg
plowing valleys into ocean floor.

☙

From blur to leopard, threshold vague. A parched
planet mourns its dearth of corn gods, its deflation
of curvature at horizon. Even photons take no oath
within a photograph. A foreign greeting swivels,
unintelligible but also familiar as the gadget
in your head, and the next thing you know,
patented. But elsewhere's a different horse,
ubiquitous for all its otherness: an opening in a cloud
where a blue top twirls, or mountains barrelling
across plains. With slow-motion catapults, evergreens
explode into consciousness, lighting up pristine
footholds in snow smooth as alpine melt. It's lonely
in the orchard so purely food.

☙

Backstreet songs can only be happened upon,
not sought. They teach grammar in a slaughterhouse,
periodically flubbing the call and response to throw off
what can't respond anyway. They blend melody
with disappearing act, singing the words that die
as surely as they endure. They salt bread, eat
rock, track Doppler effects from popped balloons. They bilk
alien pages of their exquisite otherness and bolster
the swag with stammering codes. They love nothing
so much as a loom on which to unravel their fondest
fabric. Never tiring of switching masks, they will
the impresario within to invite a lapsed movie extra
centre stage and let him spin.

☙

A motif rises for air. Maps crave starting points,
but legends drift. A meteorite smashes floor
after floor. I seek variety in fields gone to seed, but weeds
merge, grafted on a common root, wafting in a continuum.
The dodgiest scheme for capture: wake
a faint memory. Name the criminal though he's rubbed
his fingerprints off and only his victims hear the memorable
tune he whistles before rubbing them out. Like the meteorite,
he plunges: beams collapse, planks crack to splinters.
What I said before seems eons ago. I should make a move
but the moment never comes. It dawdles in a stairwell composing
roundabout chords that fool harmony into logic elusive
as owls at noon. Landings link to buttons, rooms
to flags, glyphs to orphans of speech who dangle
at the end of their words, doing what they fondly believe,
believing the words they fondly mince, secure
in habits that revive the moment they surface,
gasping for air.

☙

Long ago I fantasized perfection, wet fingertip
in air for a quick escape downwind. I thought geometry
paralleled life, except for unreal arcs and points awkwardly
cross-referenced. I liked to believe things drenched
in pigment but knew I was wrong unless
I could find the right proportion: two suspended
liquids to one target. Liquid boiled, bubbles burst
their pithy lives into swarms drifting into the open.
Seductive colours drenched whatever plot
played at the matinee. In one scene, lava flowed over
typewriters typing the rest of the plot. I thought uncertainty
a fog, but it glowed. It read the mind and filed reports
of perjury, dragged a red herring through babbling
voices, spattered paltry notes on a staff
to re-invent music. It was a start.

Acknowledgements

Special thanks to Jiří Novák and Phil Hall, whose fine sense of timbre, cadence, and *le mot juste* guided the editing of *Looms*.

I'm grateful to the following editors of magazines, who published some of the poems in *Looms*, in some cases in earlier versions:

Damian Ward Hey and Mike Russo (*And/Or*), Katia Grubisic (*Arc Poetry Magazine*), John Goodman (*ditch*), Hugh Beim-Steinberg (*Eleven Eleven*), The *filling Station* Collective, Joel Dailey (*Fell Swoop*), PJ Nights (*From East to West*), Anny Ballardini (*Poets' Corner*), Scott Howard (*Reconfigurations*), Derrick Tyson (*Sinescope*), Rupert Loydell (*Stride*), Martha Nichols and Carol Dorf (*Talking Writing*), Paul Vermeersch (*They Will Take My Island* series), Lucas and Amber Warren (*Wonk*)

to the publishers of the following chapbooks, where some of these poems first appeared:

rob mclennan of Above/Ground Press (*If Leaf, Then Arpeggio*)
Charles Alexander of Chax Press (*Magnus Loop*)

and to the following hosts of reading series and radio programs where I first read many of the poems in *Looms*, as well as the kind people who welcomed me into their homes during my reading tours:

Paul Casey, Margaret Christakos, John Herbert Cunningham, Cathy Eisenhower, Jennifer K. Dick, Roger Farr, Erin Foley, Christopher Fritton, Donna G., Liz Howard, Charlie Huisken and Jesse Huisken, Bruce Kaufmann, Michael Kelleher and Lori Desormeaux, Trisha Low, Aaron Lowinger, Shannon Maguire, Max Middle, Sachiko Murakami, Lillian Necakov, Tricia Postle, Larry Sawyer, Eric Schmaltz, Jordan Scott, Susan Evans Shaw, James Sherry, Zoë Skoulding, Dale Smith, Rod Smith, Kaegan Sparks, Dean and Françoise Steadman, Nathan Thompson, Scott Thurston, Georgia Webber, and Damian Weber.

For their support of the writing and completion of this book, I'm grateful to Brick Books (for a Writers' Reserve grant), the Ontario Arts Council, and the City of Toronto through the Toronto Arts Council.

The Author

Poet and collage artist Camille Martin grew up in Lafayette, Louisiana. A classical pianist from an early age, she earned a Master of Music degree from the Eastman School of Music. She lived for many years in New Orleans, earning an MFA in Poetry from the University of New Orleans and a PhD in English from Louisiana State University. She has resided in Toronto since 2005.

Looms is Martin's fourth book of poetry. A chapbook of poems from this collection was published as *If Leaf, Then Arpeggio* (Above/Ground Press, 2011). Her previous books are *Sonnets* (Shearsman Books, 2010), *Codes of Public Sleep* (BookThug, 2007), and *Sesame Kiosk* (Potes & Poets, 2001).

Martin blogs about poetry at http://rogueembryo.com. Her website is http://www.camillemartin.ca.

CPSIA information can be obtained at www.ICGtesting.com
Printed in the USA
LVOW100920240812

295686LV00001B/5/P